ÁRTE MONTALVO

by Mont Martin-Montalvo

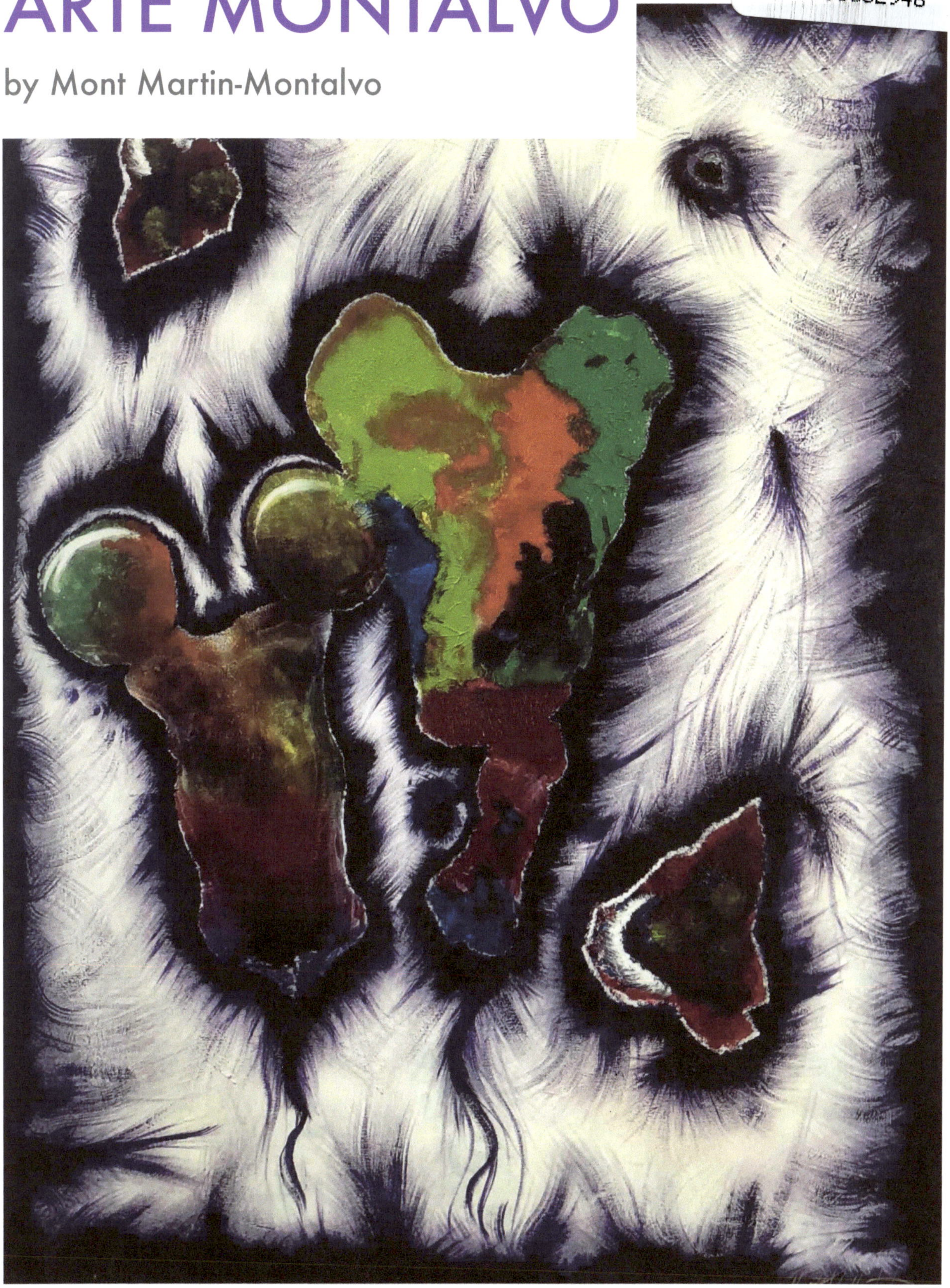

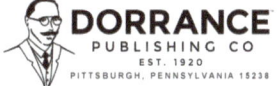

DORRANCE
PUBLISHING CO
EST. 1920
PITTSBURGH, PENNSYLVANIA 15238

Dorrance Publishing Co
585 Alpha Drive
Suite 103
Pittsburgh, PA 15238
Visit our website at www.dorrancebookstore.com

ISBN: 978-1-6470-2329-4
eISBN: 978-1-6470-2805-3

FOR MOM, WITH LOVE

Dearest:

The art of being a woman manifests in her integrity and strength. It is her ability to understand and smile under adversity. You are celebrated by God. Your actions and influence transcends; hence stands a powerful woman, inspiring and aspiring, steadfast, and loving.

Thank you kindly for the blessing of my life inclusively. Without your instilled values, without your life, this wouldn't be possible.

Thank you, Kandi, for validating and bringing forth challenges, inspiration and awakening my senses to what is true and important.

Thank you, heroes whom battle, the pandemic with fervor and dedication.

Words aren't enough.
Mont.5

SUEÑO

Amidst a glowing blue moon, beyond its reflection.

The waves as the moonlight, my thoughts inflecting.

Where could thou be? Perhaps somewhere yonder.

All through the nights, my thoughts just ponder.

Pensive of you on this bright starry night.

My spirit suddenly experiencing fright.

Sadly, my love, it isn't so bad, reflecting within, like a lost lonely lad.

Suddenly realizing, you were never mine.

Your love always scattered, like stars amidst time.

Sleep sweet angel, sleep and rest now.

For the light in the morning will bring love abound.

M.M-M

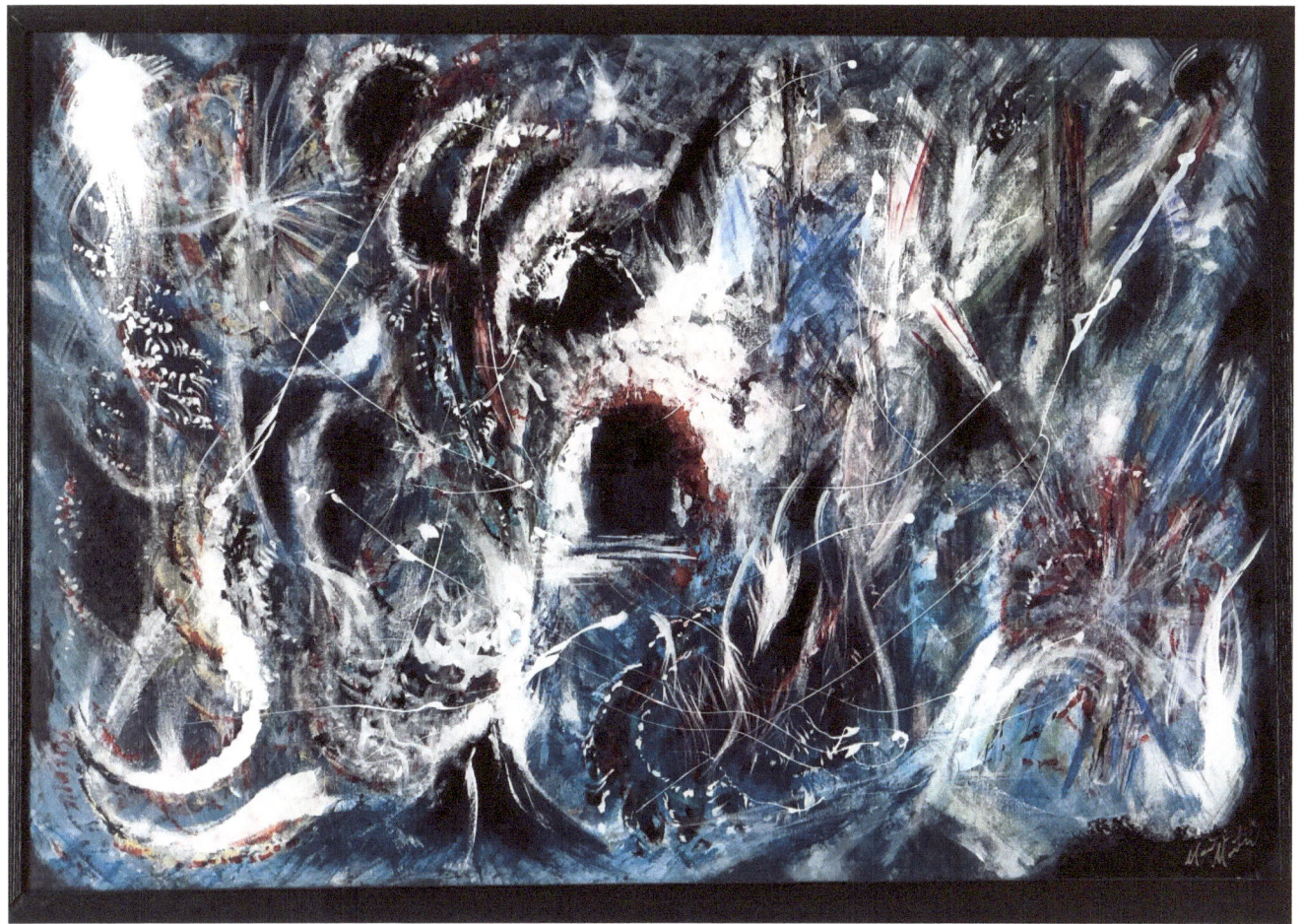

TEMPESTAD

She asked me to paint something; Leaving the canvas and essential art tools, she tuned into Pandora's Box app.

Beethoven, Tchaikovsky, Mozart and 432 frequencies filling the air; one splash after the other, rhythmically pasting the souls in a dance.

A sea of love, orbs, angels, ocean waves, and earth creatures render a storm of the senses morphing before the presence of each beholder.

Not one revelation is identical, hence the mind's eye. 3'x4'.

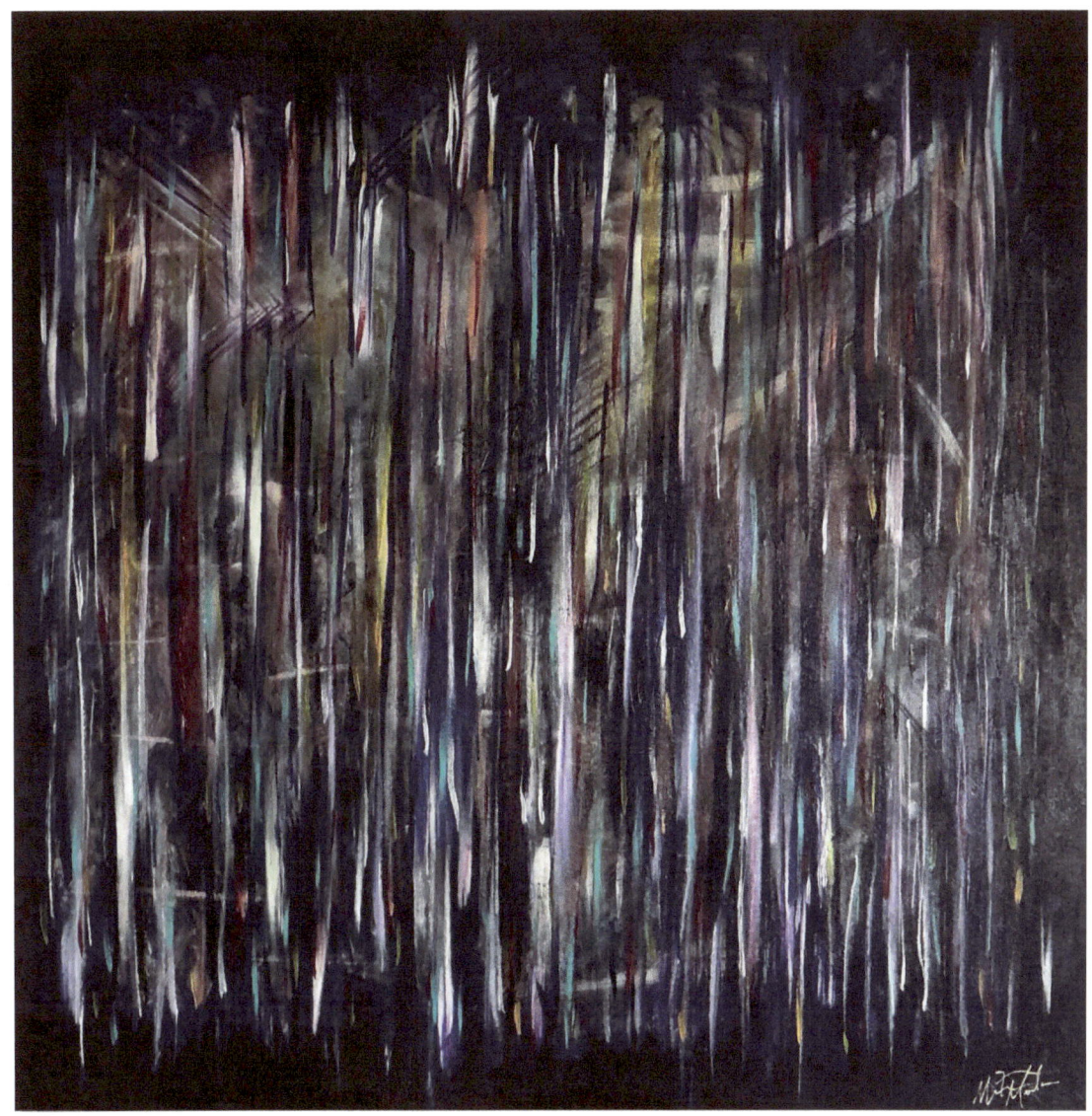

RAIN-LLUVIA

It began in a Zen room, meditating to Eastern Asian music, the brush strokes emerged a beautiful tropical flowery pattern.

Unfulfilled, the quest continued in the seeking of meaningful expression.

The consistency of strokes yielded a purplish rain, transcending beyond the realm and exposing souls yearning to peer into our reality.

Only a test of time will manifest to each viewer, the souls peering from beyond. 3'x3'.

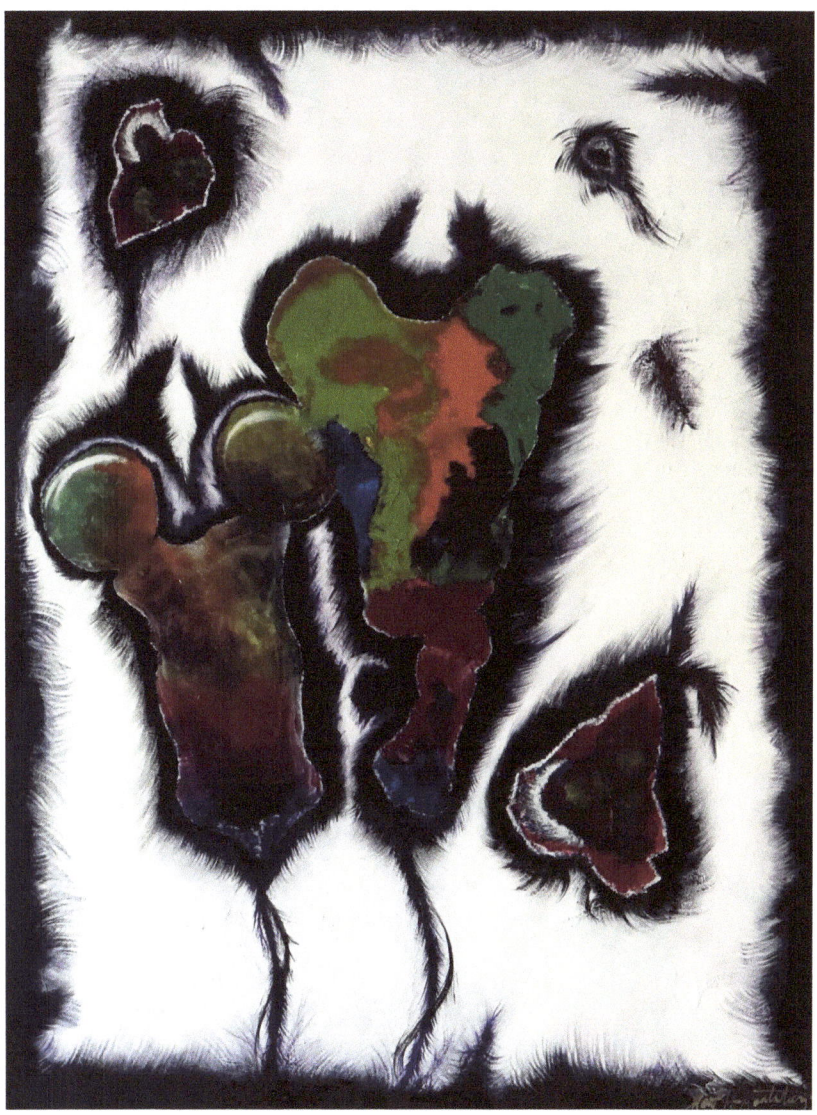

SOULMATE

Playful, daring, and witty.

Exploring the senses, shedding inhibition, and embracing the sensuality of the human form.

I am thus surrendering to love, and lust plastered onto a kaleidoscope of subtle colors indicative of the timid and yet daring essence of being human.

Dare not to question your expansive mindsets in actions, for wisdom's attained through the experiential evolutionary process of the spirit. 3'x4'.

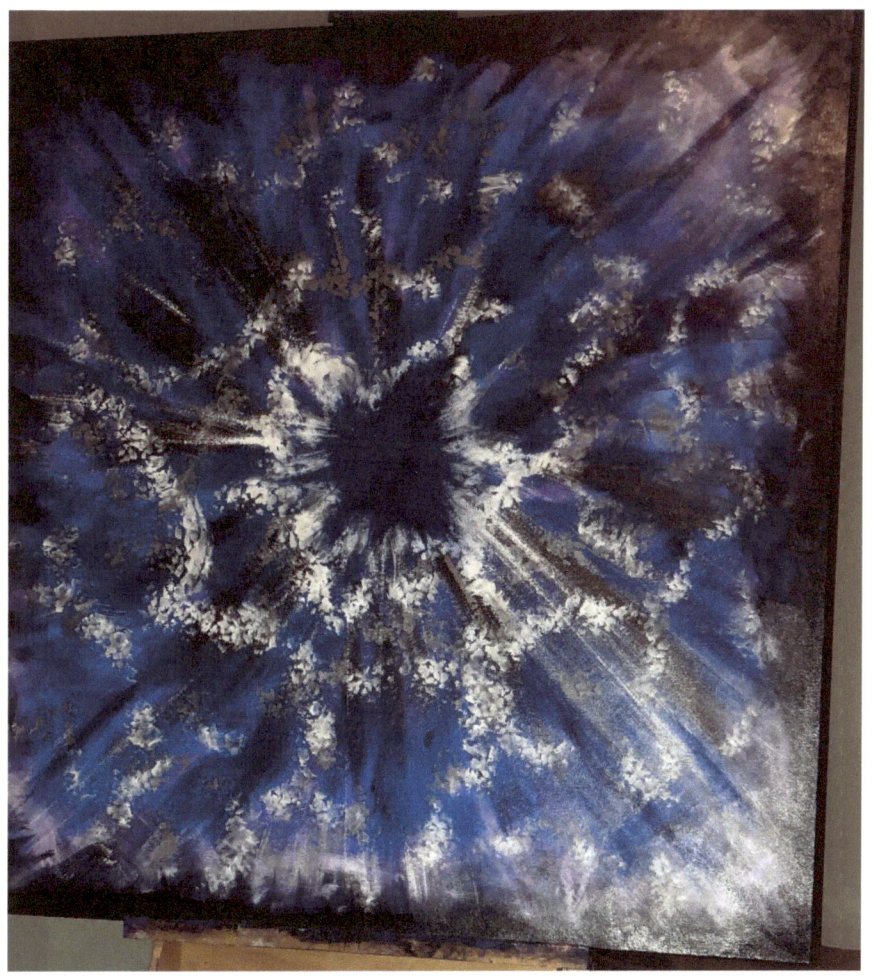

TRANSCENDED LOST

Transcended, lost in the annals of childhood memories for eternity.

An attempt to capture the mind's eye in a distant impression failed at its own worst critic.

A glimpse of a future depiction from a distant past? Perhaps time captivated in limbo.

Yet a distant past tense need to be replaced by the mind to ensure the transcendence of the spirit in individual maturity and evolution.

Look forth beyond your future and be present today in the moment. 3'x3'.

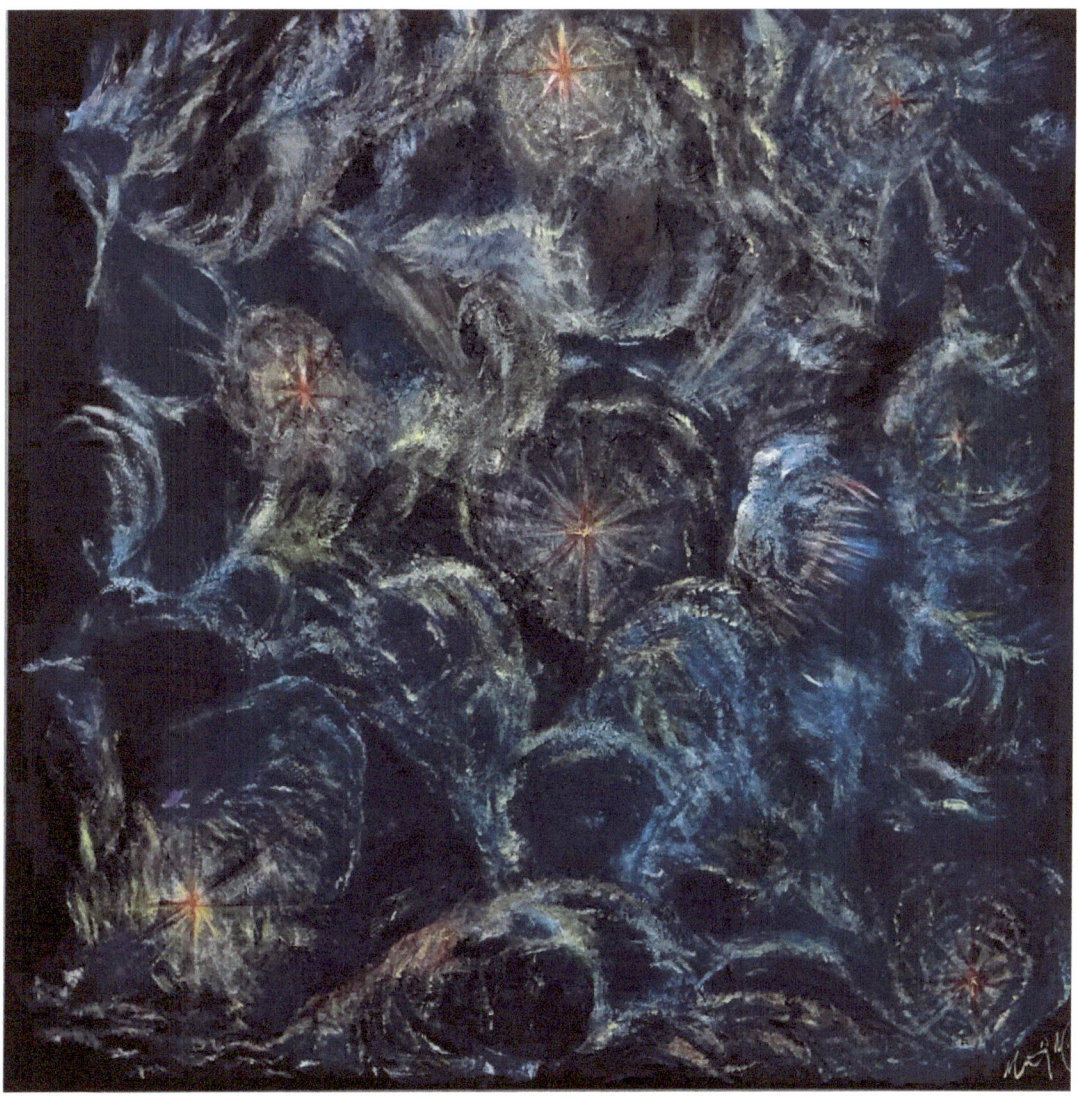

UNIVERSAL TRANSCENDENCE

Emanating from the mind's eye, and transcendence lost;

In a quest for a meaningful memory, it transcends a universal cluster of lights and clouds.

The journey is a loss, the destination unknown. The unknown is feared to whom are asleep.

Awaken yourselves from the human construct and illusion of time.

Thus, time is tangible, for time is infinite like a circle without its beginning or end. 3'x3'.

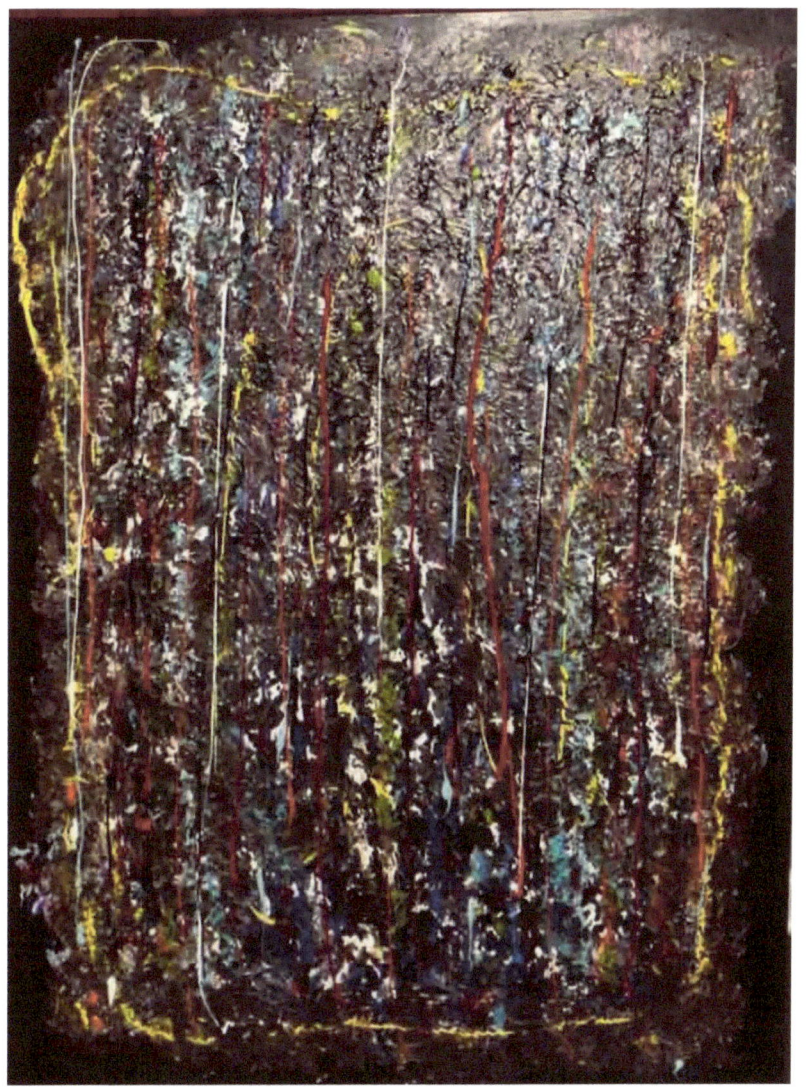

BRAILLE

Braille speaks to the soul via tactile.

Bright, linear, drunken melding colors awaken the sense of touch and proximate visual stimuli in a blink of an eye.

The visionary quest stems from eroded canyons and gullets bursting with colors.

Its valleys, invisible to the naked eye, speak via the language of Braille for all to see, touch, and discover.

The essence is such as the secrets held by a woman's heart. 3'x4'.

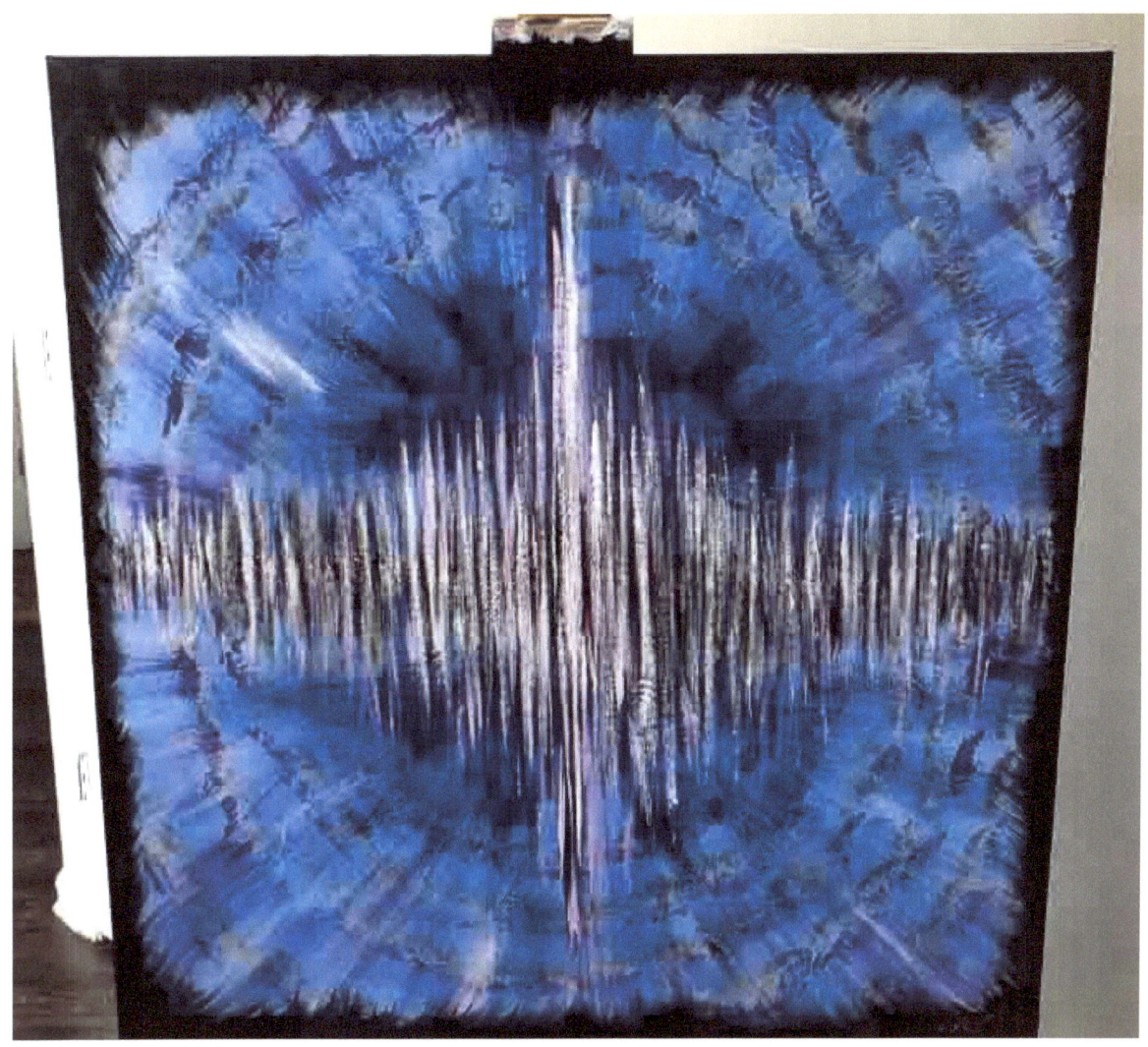

THE WELCOMING - LA BIENVENIDA

When he died, he saw a bright flash of light, but then, there was immediate darkness, followed by pitch blackness, inclusive of an awakening of all human senses.

The scent of death instills fear onto the unawaken mind.

One thing remains after a renewed promise of life: a faint memory capturing the unexplainable event in the mind, and an assurance of the possibilities of a certain grandeur.

As long as there is a breath of life within, there remains hope, and with hope, all is possible. 3'x3'.

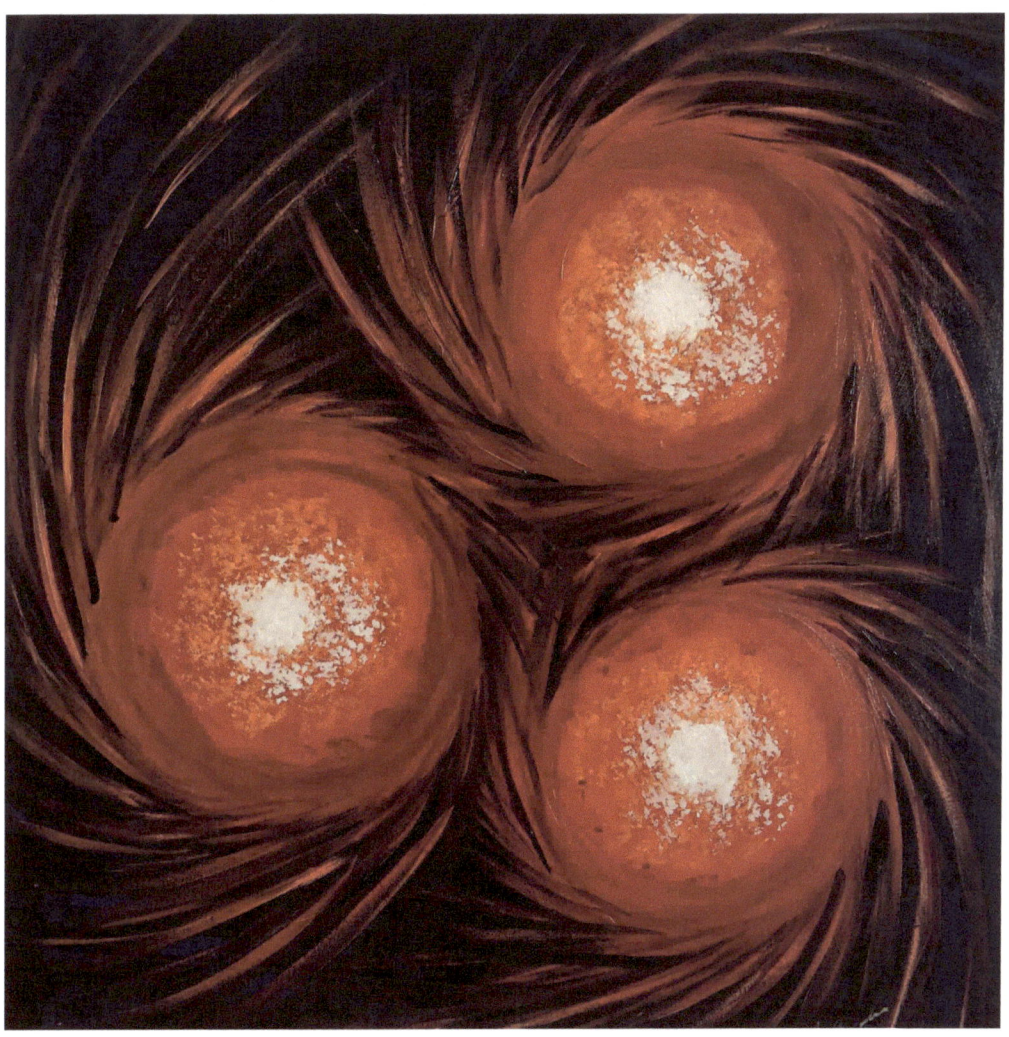

MICHÄELO - MICHAEL

I painted a firestorm, and upon naming it, thus manifested Michael.

Behold a storm is quickly approaching.

Every time I close my eyes, rushing balls of fire flash before me, hurdling into the deepest part of my mind and past my soul. Inevitable to elude, it has been with me since I recall.

The living fire, representing the archangel, is the very essence of God. Perhaps it is the universe, the sun, or merely the occipital lobe of the visual cortex processing given data.

The manifestation of light, hence, is summoned with ease.

The anomaly shall not pass but be within my being for eternity. 3'x3'.

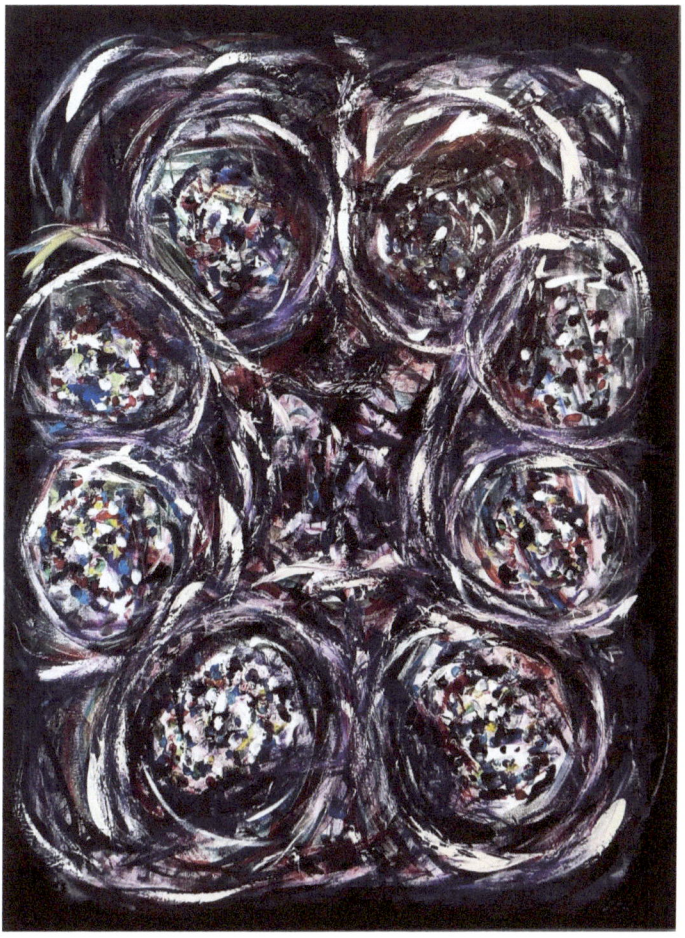

MUJÉR - WOMAN

I am thinking of the female form, in the feminine way of thinking.

Pensive, filled with desire and frustration, tunneling colors captures a subtle lustfulness.

I am angry at her complex form of thinking and understanding.

The abstractness is as mystical, ethereal, effervescent, sensual, and conceptual as the women essence.

Designed by a godly nature to be accepted, understood, loved, and listened to in its pure form.

The enigma is to have been lusted and desired by many incapables of comprehending or appreciating her intuitive nature. 3'x4'.

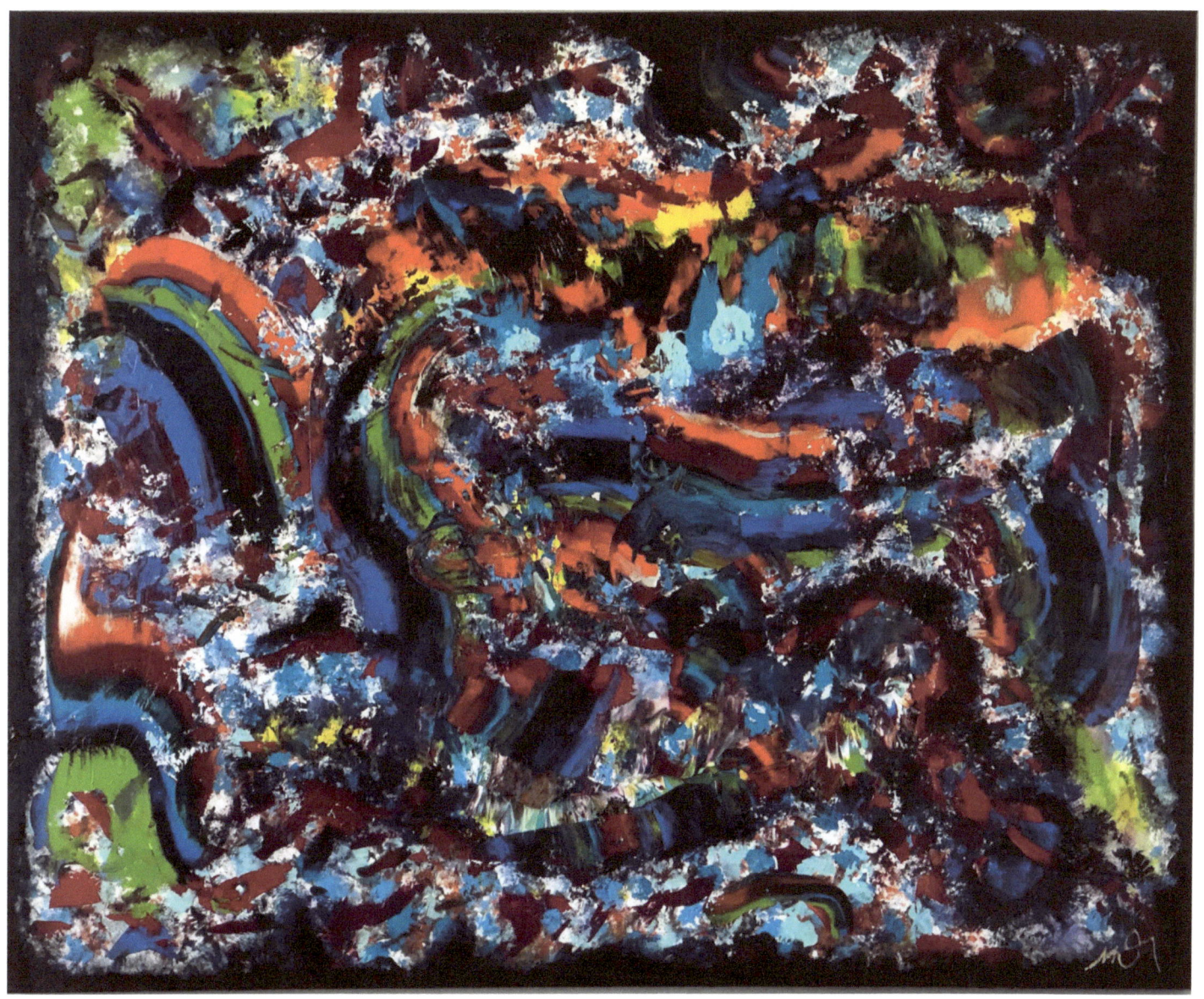

SENSUALITY - SENSUALIDADES

Free me of my inhibitions, o' wise love;

Spread and plaster my body, inclusive of my soul in an archaic prismatic medley of color representing my youth, ambition, lust, love, and promiscuity in a spectral dance.

An awakening of the senses manifests themselves in the mundane dance, thus leaving traces within the soul of the moments captured within time and space, eternally imprinted in the fabric of life, lustfulness, and love.

For what is life without dance, without music, or love? 4'x5'.

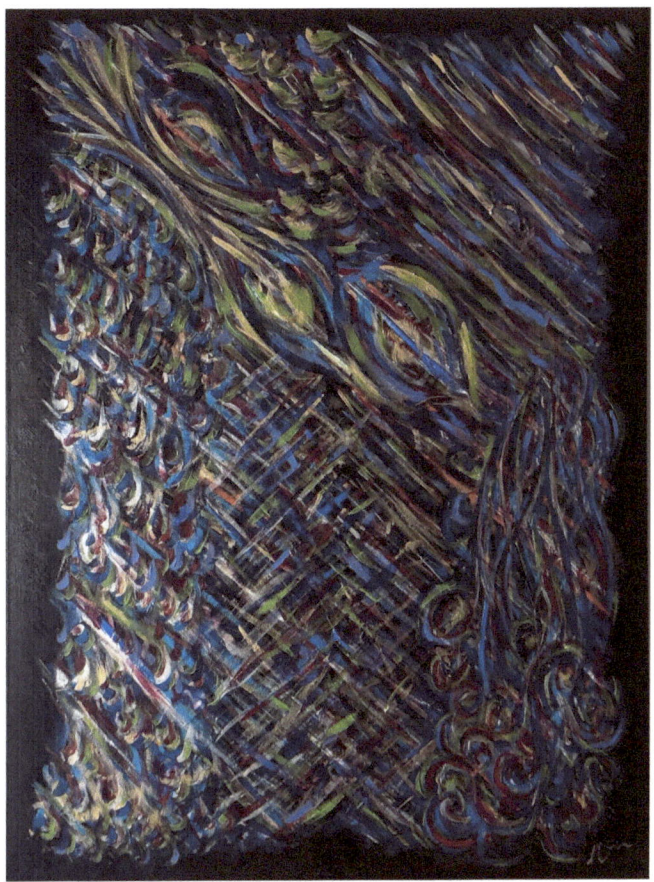

INTROSPECCIÓN - THE ART OF INTROSPECTION

A meditative search deep within the soul exposes and releases attributes, thus enhancing the spirit.

In this journey, I find anger, pain, and triggers against hostile and inhuman acts committed against the spirit.

Yet I am but the observer, I am nothing, and nothing is everything; hence everything is me. I am.

Acknowledging the hidden aspects of this virtue allows one to be free in the art of being present, thus introspecting an array of colorful abstracts conveying that which is meaningful to anyone who chooses to be accountable in the moment.

Joy, pain, sorrow, love, and happiness now flow like rivers of teardrops falling from the sky 3'x4'.

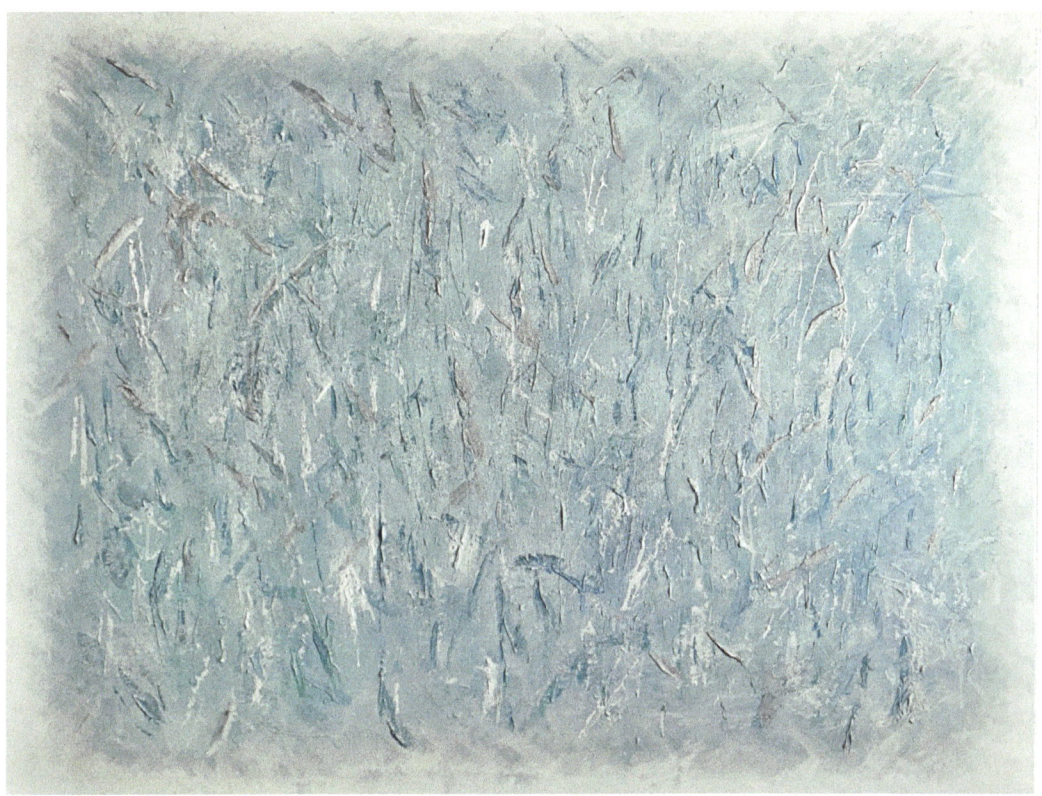

GLACIER – GLACIARES

The heart has chosen to be frozen, albeit warmed with a hue of tenderness and love.

It repeatedly chooses to remain petrified as a glacier when threatened with the imaginary neglect of its' mind, thus concealing its' true pain.

The once soluble solution will someday liquify from its solid frigid state when the collective thinking decides to do so, and when it does, be prepared; For what you will find at its core will be the hidden truth of the self.

Yet glaciers remain as a test of time.

Like the mind and heart, hence, will remain frigid in a solid-state. Much like an immense fortress wall enduring, withering, and withstanding the influential elements of a perceived fire until the end of time.

Love is warm, accept and love thyself.

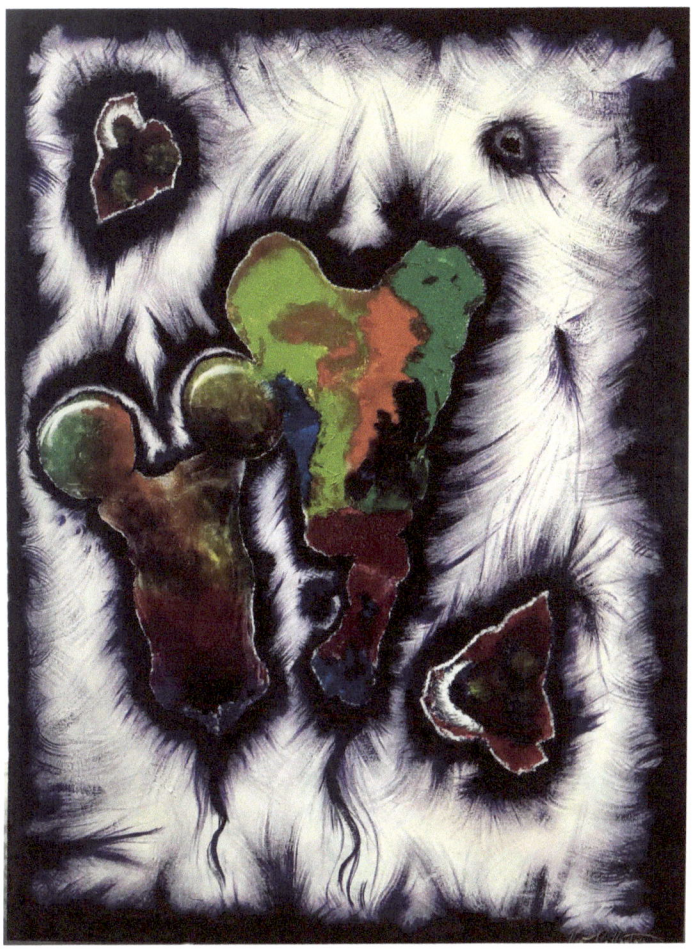

SOULMATE - LOST

Soulmate lost, the book cover print inspired by motion, love, and witty playfulness.

It is best at times to silence the mind and listen to the voice within.

It is wise to resist external variables and remain intact from their personal influences.

Influence yields distractions, and with such, your true purpose will stall and wither in manifesting itself.

Seek deep within being present in your moment and know that not all is lost.

Deny yourself the individualistic egocentrism of your created world and strike a balance within, thus bonding spiritually in love.

Know love, know love within, and you shall know thyself in pure form. 3'x4'

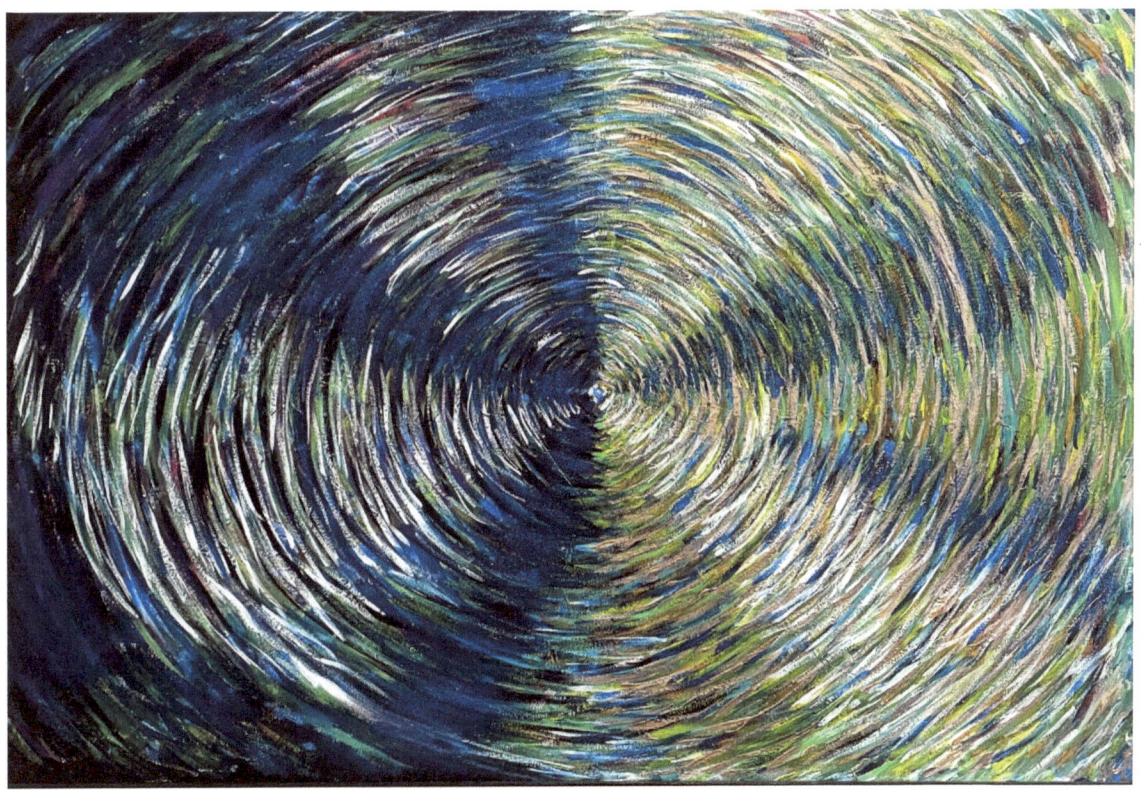

LUDICROUS – RIDICULA

Farcical, laughable, absurd, and foolish.

These are the spirals of success, doom and betrayal.

Ensnarement manifests via spiraling words, actions, emotions, and self-serving devotions, intentional or not.

Situational matters in mundane tasks vortex the spirit onto perceived success and or failure. Is this a game?

Sometimes, these are of an external locus.

It is merely what we have created out of pity for the misfortunate at their perceived disposition.

The tangible and spiritual balance yields my restoration. 3x4

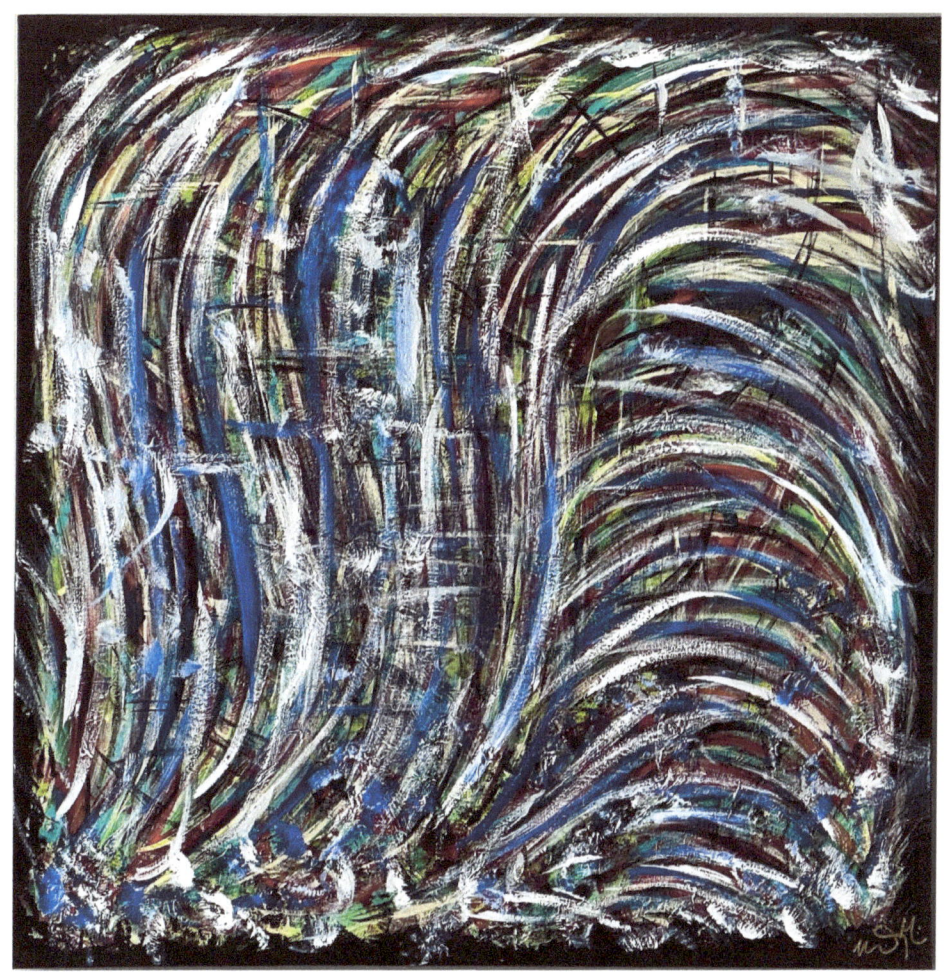

LAS OLAS – THE WAVES

Friendliness dwells in your shallowness, and in such manifest's a danger.

It is your friend amidst deep oceans, yet the deep oceans are inseparable by the tornadoes of the soul.

The shallowness protrudes a lengthy dwell, a systematic kinetic force within its longitudinal wavelength increasing with such power and fury designed to cut through the hardest diamonds.

It pretends to be friendly, yet it is, as it may save your life amidst corals, by gently placing you on soft soil.

Nonetheless, ride the crest; It is your only safe choice in the unpredictable.

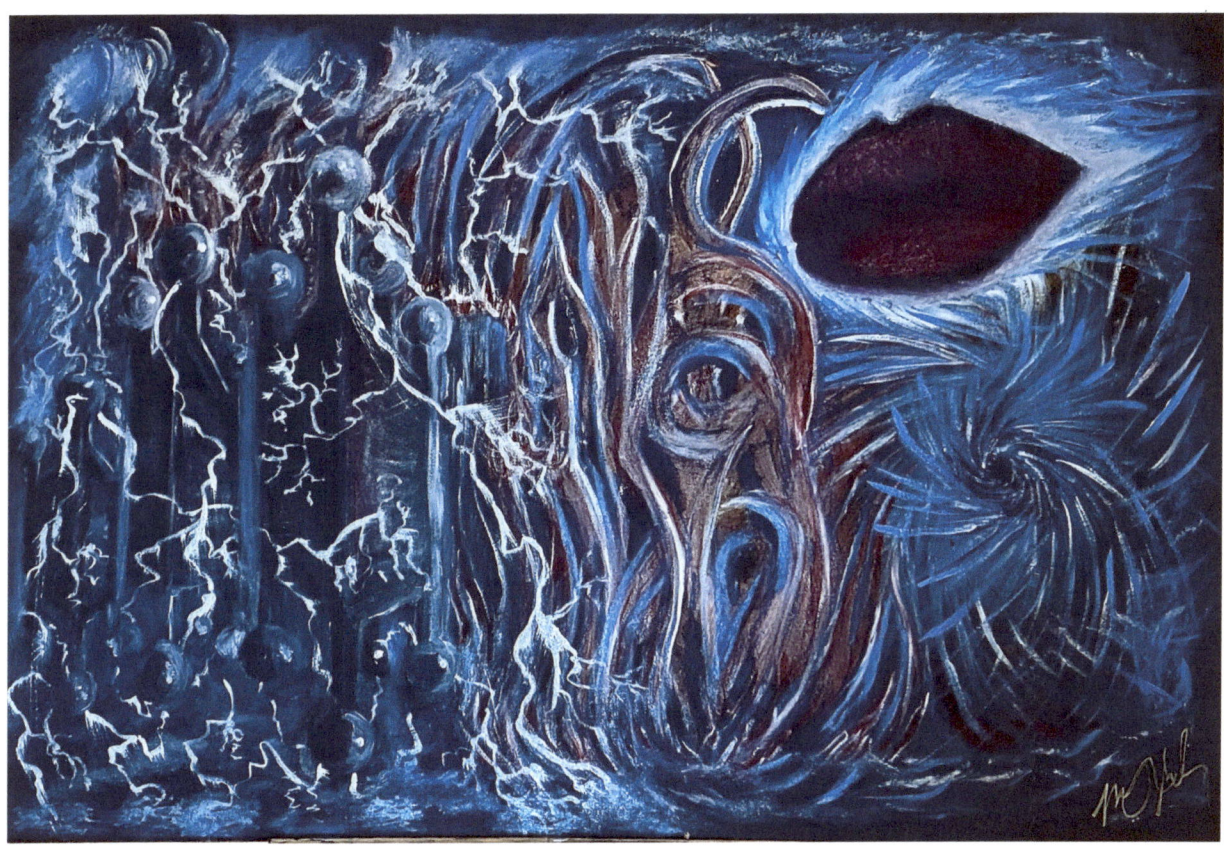

THE DREAM – EL SUEÑO

In the beginning, there was life, yet life was as a dream.
Memories faded, yet situations imprinted, thus remaining etched into the deepest
parts of the human spirit.
A pleasant sleep, disrupted again by the sound of steel, being molded upon a fire.
A machine, heavy laden, yet light as a feather.

Thunderous echoes, of the unknown, awakened in sorrow and comforted with love
expressible in this realm.
It is the unknown within you, yet familiar enough as known threats.
The lure, lust, and dancing in fiery waters are sure to save or consume you.

But this is a dream, as with life, all is illusory, for what is real is pure light, love within.
Yet if yours is infernal, let it be so, if only for a season.
For you also will emerge renewed; awakened if only for a season, once again in
this realm, surrounded and comforted by true love within.